Ever the Sky

poems by

Ada Pendill

Finishing Line Press
Georgetown, Kentucky

Ever the Sky

For Hollie

Publisher: Leah Huete de Maines
Editor: Christen Kincaid
Cover Art and Design: Ada Pendill
Author Photo: Ada Pendill

Order online: www.finishinglinepress.com
also available on amazon.com

Author inquiries and mail orders:
Finishing Line Press
PO Box 1626
Georgetown, Kentucky 40324
USA

Contents

Ever More Stars

I have known you
Like a mountain knows the sky.
Together we are touch and spine
And no star has been on fire
Nor has a river cried
For as long as your soul
Has danced with mine.

Quantum, entangled, alive—
Our electrons orbit,
Galaxies intertwined.
Spooky action at a distance,
Still, we close the space:
Words on a park bench,
In my car,
And through the dialogue of skin.

The sun will burn five billion years.
Then you will wake me
To witness the final light.
That moment—like this one—
Will be coated in gold,
And we will surrender to the dark
As we did to the first light, so long ago.

I want to teach you to lose your fear
Of the vast and starry sky
And help me remember
That Earth is where we stand.
Andromeda, the Moon, the ground.
The Bird singing outside simply *is*—
The same as my Anam Cara and me.

Emeralds, Gold, and Honey

Through the emerald distance of my window
Zwischen ich und du—
Signals, signs, and ciphers
Glide like grateful weary birds,
Returning wiser from the icy blue.

I'll shake this spun candy from my head,
You'll aspire to greater deeds.
We two will purge our gold of lead
And watch the horizon intertwined,
Eager surfers watching hope rise in the line.

This slight crack,
Where it's said the light gets in—
I will eat its rays for breakfast,
You'll bathe unguarded in its glow,
Unready for the secrets of the day.

Our honey drips slowly.
Shoes of stone, skirts of glue.
We would have devoured this road already,
Were it not so coy—
But once tamed, it could yield the sweetest prize.

Shipwreck Sunrise

Her side of the bed
became the perfect place
to keep poetry books and tissues.

They floated on the comforter
like shards of a shipwreck
bobbing just beyond
the hungry ocean's reach.

And I was always certain
that I had drowned.

Maybe life shouldn't be so hard,
unlike falling in love—
so easy,
where all you do
is look over the edge
and let go.
Maybe life itself
should be fallen into
in just the same way.

But my life had teeth
and had turned feral,
too many roads unfurling
in every compass direction.
Too many moon-like changes,
so much skin left to shed.
And so of course
my bed with her became an ocean
that ravaged and sank the ship.
And maybe the life I lived
had no choice
but to be so hard.

And now you,
my tiny flame of orange
peeking over the line
where the ocean meets the sky.
Birds dance in the air
where your glow begins to shine.
Even the air seems to know
that you have arrived.
And so does the island
whose edge I've been looking for
and now I can finally see
as its beach reflects you—
a soft welcome, finally, for me.

Horizonized

I was saved by my contraption of hope
By my tightrope walker's eyes.
I was a lump of lead, held aloft
By the thinnest sketch of a line.
The sky, unfazed by my strange weight,
Dealt with me like just another cloud.

Bravery is blind, a newborn foal.
Ignorant, confident, and willfully thick.
Syrup-like. Insistent, with a certainty
That the ground beneath our feet
Held no claim on us—
I was but a stray floating feather.

Parallel universes, oranges, popcorn—
They all open, if you know the way.
But you, you were a chapter in a book
And as I spread your delicate pages
And read your words carved into the rain,
My heart broke free of the shore.

Like a drummer, sweating—pounding,
Or a dancer slicing the air,
Singing sweetly
Through the light voice of her feet
For the eager ears of the wooden floor—
I'll be with you in moonlit rhymes.

This is where I'd like to make my home,
Where the little things that are wrong
Become what holds the most appeal.
I have been paid for waiting for you.
It is time to live on earth again,
Wrapped in the arms of its gravity.

This is Thus

Treasure smoke, figment.
Realer and untethered—you, butterfly, you.
Now we know:
wherever we are,
together
is the island we seek.

Rain—the tears of memory—
blanket cortex,
trickles down neuron streams.
Plastic minds carve new paths,
mapped
to never un-know each other again.

Secret signals, mystical.
Creator of now,
moment-machine churning—
force of feathers, gravity of softness—
assuaged.
Buried deep,
for you to gently seek.

Make a Wish

Why can't we remember being born?
Was it that the lightning and thunder
Of that day was so terrifying?
Or just so amazing that the rest of life
Would seem like flowers that never bloom
If we knew or could remember
That first breath and first light?

Gratitude holds hands with this moment.
May I live at ease, be happy, at peace -
A meditation that never comes easy.
We light the little fires and sing the song
And the smoke from birthday candles
Carries secret wishes up to the gods.
What they do from there is unknown.

I was born with something,
Though it wasn't the original sin.
And the stars that were carefully arranged
That night my heart was wound
So that it might start its clocklike ticking,
Were placed a little differently
For me than for you.

Without the smell, look, and feel of time
Today would be just another day.
But today insists on being more.
The universe prefers to live alone,
So ease is not its gift to you.
But a trip around the sun, a simple circle,
Takes us far, though we never move at all.

We're Off to See

A brain.
A heart.
Courage.
Three is the magic number—
no more,
no less.

The secret of the universe
is that it diminishes us all:
from the mighty sun
to the tiniest bug.

From Infinity's mouth
A lava of scale pours
We run—
so fast, so far—
and with every step,
we shrink.

Insignificance-generator.
Minuscule-maker.
Tiny-grinder.

I felt these machines hum inside me
when I was a child
and was told
there are no walls,
no edge
to the velvet black
and its twinkling stars.

My budding mind—
small already—
collapsed to nothing
as I tried to drift from Earth
until I touch a wall
that would never be there.

Illusions of the String

I flew this year like it was a kite
And you were the blue of the sky.
Birds and tornadoes
Know less about wind
Than I knew that day.

But now your blue is fading
And the light that danced
With the thin skin of the year—this kite,
Has spun off to find other partners.

And so here is that moment
When the day teeters,
And the purple mist of night
Sneaks in through the cracks
Of the now orange-juice sky
With scars gouged by planes
like a game of tic tac toe
two angels might play
And soon the hot snowflakes
Of well-placed stars
Begin to land gently
Across the now deep black sky.

And our minds,
Eager to make sense
Of anything
Dropped by the cat at our door
See in the sky
Stories and figures,
Pots and pans
And over there twins,
Not far from the hunter
With his spangled dagger
In his spangled belt.

And that's what I do,
Right now,
With this dotted year
As it comes close to sleeping.
What was it exactly?
Here in its night,
Sprinkled with flames.
What do I think it meant
Or what do I think it means?
Maybe that it was everything
While being nothing at all.

So fly away birds.

And tornadoes, be gone.

Scalpel Dawn

I know the Bodhi and the Lotus.
The chrysalis and the flower's bud—
They see me as I see them,
On the eve before the change.

I hear the words that once lingered
On feathered winds that flew
From my heart to those deep places
Where I knew me—and you knew you.

No scalpel could hunger so deeply,
Nor any surgeon's eyes be so clear
As to find the part of me that bleeds
In the way the empty husk once knew.

I will wake with a new body
And glow in that quiet, heavy way I do.
And I will be a tree for you to ponder under
Or be your flower that thrives in dirty water.

Mark my words with small pink flags
That waving against the slab-blue sky
And know this earth is only clay
And my body yearns to learn its ways.

Tut, Tut, it Looks Like Rain

These summer nights
   When the sky becomes a lake
And jolts of lightning drown the lights
      In watertight houses
Where nothing ever happens

The sky's diamonds
   Huddle in puddles,
Exhausted from clinging to their mothers—
      Their airtight clouds
   Where everything had to happen

I am your umbrella,
   As thin a shield as shields can be
   So I made a pact with the storm-lit sky
And signed my name on the horizon line
That you might get wet, but will always dry

    And
  on
   that
     I give
  my
    word

The Wash and Buzz

You, the keeper of bees—
Queen of stings.
I have dialed my radio,
my ancient radio,
all night, from low to high
while static fills my mind.

I am like the watercolors
I torture myself with.
Tubes of frustration,
flowing rivulets I cannot reign.
Signal-less and noise-full,
but nonetheless, I try.

Us, such a small word, like lemon yellow
dabbed by water onto paper
can just be made out—
a mere ghost at dawn—
or maybe like a heartbeat
manifesting beneath the paint.

I See You

I see you like no other.
Free of the metal that was
Hammered, blown, and fired
And fashioned into devices
To keep your wings asleep
And your voice, boxed, forgotten.

I am one with your wave
And together we throw circles
Begetting more in widening rings
Of concentric hope and dreams
From snow of North, to heat of South
We will orbit what we have become.

I am golden and you are a pearl
Forged from Earth's mass
And we will have the strength of the sun
Its fire eternal as it moves
Through cold, empty paths
Shrouded in void and dust.

And Time will look in wonder
At what she sees in us—
Two points of joy and awe
Transcendent of her ancient power;
Two trees still with green leaves
Where spring no longer reaches.

My Mother's Song

I save tickets from places and shows I attend
In a box from my mother's girlhood.
That old box is one of the things that remain.

I save tickets to remember my life,
Though I forget how it started,
Or why I chose this way to hold on.

I could have written lines like these instead—
Breadcrumbs to find my way back,
To recall, one day, my mother.

But my mother won't live in the future,
So, I chase a regret I can't quite erase—
Why did I never write about her like this?

In the box, beside my clutter of ticket stubs,
Lies a pouch holding her old charm bracelet,
From the days when she was young:

Twenty charms that tinkle along the chain—
States she visited, Cypress Gardens,
Tiki idols, St. Louis Zoo, Harrison High, Honest Abe.

My mother's memories sparkle more than mine.
The jingle of metal plays like a song—
And through that music, I know her—
In a way I won't forget.

A Very Happy 4th of July

Don't take the sun lightly
or you'll get a sunburn,
or worse—those wings
you worked so hard on
might melt.

And never forget—
the line between
fireworks and thunder
is thinner than it looks.
Even Buddy knows that.

And another about fireworks—
they're no grander
exploding in the sky
than they are when two
hold sparklers in their hands.

Buddy can't read poems,
so I'll buy him a thunder jacket—
a way to remember me
when storms come and I'm not there.
I will buy you one too.

When the rain pounces and pours
and your corn on the grill
can't be rescued,
remember there is always
more corn.

And remember that trash cans
have feelings too
and when the rain builds rivers
where the streets used to be
yours might jump in and flee.

And the next morning
if something is beeping
from a mysterious alarm
take a deep breath,
then find it and put it to sleep again.

Remember—the 4th of July
can come any time, even the 3rd of May.
Whether you shake from thunder
or laugh in the rain,
the choice is yours—always.

The Mesh Between

Waking slowly to a wooded morning.
Birds telling each other about their dreams
Or all of the things they have to do today.
The silence between their chirps
Settling on me like a cool, damp blanket
As the air prepares for the warmth of the sun.

Stiff from sleeping on the ground
In a tent, camping with my youngest child.
Grateful for the words the campfire summoned,
the quiet joy this moment breathes.
How thin the tent's mesh felt last night,
between us and the trees, the stars.

We Can Only Jump So High

And it made me wonder, clinging to this gravity,
Just how much does our little planet weigh?
What would be needed for the calculation—
All the dogs, and houses, and mice,
And TVs, phones, cars, and chocolate bars?

I feel it in my bones that the Earth is heavy,
Obeying ancient laws of pull and spin.
And who outside of us would care
How our small, dense rock compares
To Alpha Centauri, the Moon, or Mars?

It weighs just enough—exactly as it should.
But I remember, as a kid, I wondered.
I wondered about many heavy things:
Like, are magic carpets discovered,
Or are they earned—or made?

Stitching the Sea

I wonder what stitches I would use
To embroider an image of your face.
I only know the Outline Stitch
The French Stitch and Satin Stitch,
The latter of which I used to stitch a heart
With three strands of bright red floss
And in which the stitches started out straight
But then veered increasingly to the left.
Even the needle, with its one good eye
Still recently poked with strands of red floss
Could see we had gone askew.
I imagine that whoever is in charge
Of stitching each beautiful wave in the sea
Knows how fluid beauty and energy can be.
So by the time I got to the other side
The heart had ended up being
Not quite as perfect
As I once hoped it would be.
But now I think the heart,
Imperfect, satin stitches,
Red floss,
Made with love,
And care and hope—

Could be,
Without another stitch,
A perfect portrait—
Of you.

Sunshine Ghosts

On a road close to home, in the noon sun,
on a short lunch break,
I see the fleeting art on the asphalt flicker.
The trees, sun, and road dance while I drive—
shadow pictures dying in my wake.

Hold your breath when you pass a graveyard
my children were taught by someone to say.
And if they were with me now at noon
in my car, that is exactly what they would do
until the last grave passes safely by.

Later they would see the decayed shrine
so small and crumbled, to remember a driver
who drove ahead and stopped forever
at the turn of a road which maybe became
a turning point for those left behind.

But my kids aren't with me today, it's just me
as I then drive under an old trestle bridge,
an old rusted span across a damp creek
where not long ago a teen chose his fate,
unable to go on, in a way I could once relate.

Finally, I arrive at a beautiful old farmhouse
which no longer hosts the dead farmer,
long gone, his name lost in the dust.
There are no ghosts here—just my therapist.
How about we talk about my childhood today?

Flames That Sing in Morning Rain

Through the steady summer morning rain
there is a bird outside my window
that continues to sing undaunted.
Or perhaps I should say I think it's defiant
because I've always imagined that the rain
snuffs out songs the way it does flames.
But this bird is seemingly singing more now
than it might if the sun weren't drowning
behind this wet gray veil.

I wonder if birds can show human spirit?
I wonder that because I sometimes do things
that are like when birds sing in the rain—
things born of the quiet alchemy
of hope and need and stubbornness.
I don't know that it's ever made the rain leave
or if it helped me to keep my feathers clean,
or kept my nest from sagging in the rain
but it keeps my mind on the worms it may bring.

And even now I hear another humanlike bird
a little ways off in another tree, showing that spirit.
But though her voice is soft and soaked
and now the rain is coming down harder
with even some rumbles of morning thunder
that little stubborn flame continues singing.
Now some more are joining the choir.
Maybe it's neither birdlike nor human
but simply the way life carries on, singing.

Four Useless Legs at the Crossroads

This bench seems at first to be just a bench,
sitting among the green leaves of trees
and keeping guard where three paths meet.

Maybe a man named Sam or Hank
decided to plant the bench in the rich soil
where the woods and the three paths meet.

Whatever the decision, the bench was here
and it had never thought to walk away
and we were grateful for that as we sat.

It is true, saving people from fires is brave
but choosing to speak of fate aloud—
that's a rare kind of bravery where three paths meet.

Maybe the bench had heard it all before
And would have sighed, if it could,
hearing another pair talking about such things.

The leaves are still green so it's too soon
for us to confront the beautifully scary future
and choices carved from loss or bliss.

So you finish crafting a heart inside a leaf
we stand, grateful for our brave indecision.
and smile as we leave the bench behind.

But the bench barely notices as we leave
among the green leaves and can only think
if it could be brave, it would pick the path to the left.

No Sunglasses Allowed in Class

One afternoon
on the Jersey Shore,
I was reminded
of the messages
a wave can bring
and how it can remind us
that power and surprise
rise from nowhere
and vanish the same.

The Universe is always thinking
and if we listen,
always revealing, always teaching,
but when through an unexpected wave
it spoke to me, I only learned
that my brand new sunglasses
had just started an unexpected journey
to Lisbon, Portugal, or more likely
swallowed by the ocean.

The Universe teaches lessons:
to savor each wave, like a surfer.
and to catch summer in jars—
the laughter, the salt, the sun—
to feed you through winter.
Or to be impressed by
the butterflies that fly
and not the ones pinned to cards.
Lessons we all should know.

And the difference between
fearlessness and fierceness
and how to know your gold
and also see the gold in others.
It's the crooked beams and scuffed floors
that make a house a home.

And those sunglasses—
lost to the sea—
never suited me at all.

Winter Song

Silver sky, lying like a wet blanket,
Like an echo of the warmth of summer sun,
Like a false rhyme,
But not a lie.

You are burrowed in alone, not far away,
To survive the poison of the north wind
Your winter skin, a husk stretched tight,
Forgetting how green the leaves can be.

Even the birds today
Have flown beyond their feathers,
Past your burrow, to more hopeful places
As I try once more to coax a simple flame.

When the Sky Blinks

A horizon line is inevitable—
physics inscribed it long ago:
where there's an earth,
there awaits a sky.

Cardinal on a branch
Flame bird popping
Against the white-blue snow.
And there is that line again.

Beat and rest, beat and rest—
the rhythm I hold onto.
Not my own, but yours—
and nothing can divide us.

This leaf, with its veins,
Green river veins, beside the next.
Then more: a green multitude—
blue sky kissing.

It's easier to walk in heels
when the horizon is steady.
But the lines between us blur.
Suddenly, we stop seeing.

No Further Than Bones

"I feel it in my bones"
Means that the heavy feelings
Sink right through our skin
To our skeletons.
The same ones that keep us
From collapsing in piles
On the cold ground.

They're the ones we use
To help us flee from fear
Or reach for joy.
And the ones that are there
Whether buried
Or burned,
The framework of being.

So when I say I feel it,
That something bad
Is well on its way,
And I feel it in my bones,
Just know I say it
Because that feeling

Has nowhere else to go.

The Month of Ghosts

This is the month of ghosts
And the year of knowing in our bones
That we won't touch the moon.
Your lemon heart,
My red apple heart,
Won't escape the clutches
Of this heavy earth.

You said you tried
With all your might, like the trees
Who clung to their green
Until the cold came in the night
Like a thief
To steal it all away.

And I tried
Like the ocean tries
To spread itself across
The world
With my water fingers
And liquid mind.

But now

We live within a crack
That was opened
Like a slight smile
On the face of the world,
The world
Of concrete and green
And frantic highways,
The wall
Between what was and what waits.

We've awoken to find
That we now live
In endless purgatorial space
Not the hush of the liminal,
But well earned,
For showing
No heed.

Better to have been birds
And to have used our wings
To find the places
The ground can't see.

Better still
What the next turn of the wheel
Might
Or might not bring.

But for now,
The once-green mouths
Of October trees
Whisper in their brown and orange piles
What time truly means.

Ada Pendill is a poet based in the Philadelphia area. With a background in visual arts, she brings a painter's sense of space and image to her writing, drawing inspiration from the natural world, visual language, and the subtle surrealism of the everyday. When not writing poetry or computer code, she spends as much time as possible with the birds and trees.

www.ingramcontent.com/pod-product-compliance
Lightning Source LLC
Chambersburg PA
CBHW022055080426
42734CB00009B/1362